Choosing a Cocker or Springer or Sprocker Spaniel

~

By

Anne-Marie Millard

&

Richard Botwright

Choosing a Cocker or Springer or Sprocker Spaniel

Copyright © 2014 Anne-Marie Millard

All rights reserved.

ISBN: **1503074730**
ISBN-13: **978-1503074736**

DEDICATION

Firstly a thank you to family, who have left me to indulge in my love of spaniels, my Mother for various dogs determined to share her duvet and pillow. My daughters for letting a pregnant snoring dog, sleep on their favourite sofa whilst they watch tv from the floor.

Next to friends and locals who do not bat an eyelid when I appear in front of them with a face splattered in mud (I don't mind if you tell me by the way). To all my mothers friends who collect newspapers for me (an essential part of puppy house training), and to Mike and Sue Parkinson (with our lovely Sprocker Johnny) who also appear at the gates with bundles of papers and news of Johnny's progress.

Thank you to all our puppy buyers who stay in touch over the years, it is so appreciated and finally to Richard, for cleaning up behind me, being a quiet voice of reason, for making everything possible and just for being him.

Choosing a Cocker or Springer or Sprocker Spaniel

CONTENTS

	Introduction	1
1	A History	3
2	The Cocker Spaniel Defined	5
3	The Springer Spaniel Defined	12
4	The Sprocker Spaniel Defined	18
5	Now The Science – Health Checks	23
6	Identifying Your Puppy	27
7	Finding Your Puppy	31
8	Preparing For Your Puppy	38
9	Living With Your Puppy	52

INTRODUCTION

This book is written from the heart and our experience of Spaniels over the years. I started with one liver and white London born Springer pup when my oldest daughter was a baby, and as the family grew so did the number of dogs living in and around the home. From having a full time job which required looking clean, juggling dogs, cats, ducks, sheep, ponies, pigs and goats, through an awful recession, a time being a single mum, to the point where we are now. This is now a lovely and lively bank of kennels, a slightly chaotic home and a life surrounded by dogs and puppies.

So I think I can safely say that the experiences over the past years has given me a rounded and sensible viewpoint on what a spaniel can do, how they can drive you towards insanity but will always, always win the day. There is nothing in the world as loving, awe inspiring, happy, clever, naughty (but nice) and just wonderful as all the spaniels out there. I am certainly not saying they are always perfect, but they have such a huge place in so many people's hearts, getting your first spaniel will change your life forever.

These days Spaniels are our life in every sense, from in the house, to out in the kennels. Here at our work 'Uggeshall Kennels' we breed now on a full time basis 'Working Spaniels', namely English Springers, Cockers and Sprockers. I am lucky enough now to have my partner Richard working by my side, his field of expertise far outweighs mine when it comes to gundogs and combining that with his entire life working with dogs, we make a rounded team of knowledge which we can hopefully impart to you.

1 A HISTORY

We first see the English physician Dr. John Caius describing the spaniel in his book the 'Treatise of English Dogs' published in 1576. This was the first mention of the differing Spaniel breeds by function. By 1891, Sydenham Edwards was explaining in the Cynographia Britannica that the 'Land Spaniel' should be split into two kinds: the Springing of Hawking Spaniel, and the Cocking or Cocker Spaniel.

At this point in time, both Cockers and Springer Spaniels were born in the same litters. The purpose at this time in their life was to serve as a hunting dog. The smaller Cockers used to hunt Woodcock, whilst their larger littermates the Springer's would 'spring' or flush the game bird into the air where a trained falcon or hawk would bring the birds to the handler.

Many Spaniel breeds were developed during the 19th century, and often named after the countries where they were developed, or after their owners (who were often nobility). Two types of spaniels were predominant and were said to have been of 'true Springer type'. These were the Norfolk and Shropshire Spaniels, and by the 1850's, they were shown under the name of the Norfolk Spaniel.

By January 1899, the Spaniel Club of England and the Sporting Spaniel Society held their trials together for the first time. Two years later, in 1902, a combination of the physical standard from the Spaniel Club of England and the ability standard from the Sporting Spaniel Society led to the English Springer being officially recognized by the English Kennel Club. The American Kennel Club followed suit in 1910.

So by now we have the Cocker and the Springer Spaniel being officially recognized. But what about the Sprocker? It is very hard to track down the roots of the Sprocker. Basically they are a cross between a Cocker and a Springer, and since in the knowledge that it had not been that long a time ago (in the grand scheme of things) that a Springer and a Cocker came from the same litter, when the Sprocker actually became officially discussed as an independent 'type' amongst the general public is hard to pin down.

The general feeling is that gamekeepers in Scotland began to breed Springers and Cockers together to produce a duel purpose working field Spaniel for their big estates, combining the best traits of their Springers crossed with a cocker. You cannot call a Sprocker a cross breed as such (unlike a labradoodle for example) since they are from the same breed. So when the Sprocker hit the highlights is difficult to exactly pin down.

However Sprockers are going from strength to strength these days, and long may that last.

2 THE COCKER SPANIEL DEFINED

It is impossible to explain every bit about a breed, simply because they are so diverse (like us). We spend a lot of time talking to people about their dogs, and listening to their tales of dogs past. There is also a lot of time spent trying to de-bunk myths about the poor spaniels, and gently persuading people that Spaniels are not 'mad' and don't need running round a race track several times a day.

'Working' spaniels does not mean that they have to 'work', obviously some do only that, some are multi-talented, being a house pet during the summer and a shooting dog during the 'season'. Others, like quite a few of ours, are just wonderful pets to have around and interact with.

What follows is a description that we have built up over the years, taking into account all of our dogs, so not just the pets and not just the working dogs. I hope you can glean exactly what you want to know from the following. I have broken it down into the male and female of each type, simply because as you will see, they are so different.

Cocker males:

Solid, determined and strong willed – all in a good way. These are little power houses of happiness. Cocker boys are entertainment on legs, short sturdy legs. But with those legs, boy can they jump!

They do need variety to keep their mind and body stimulated and to blow off some steam. However taking our two boys into account, they are very good at exercising themselves, running in their natural hunting pattern of a loop, bouncing back to just check where you are and, happy with all being well, off they go again. Once they have had their moments of charging around, they are then fantastic at just settling down and snoozing off.

Being such great family pets, they don't really like being left alone for too long. So although they don't need hours of exercise (and in fact as long as they have a loo break, having a day off a walk is not too awful every now and then) they do need company. So if you are going to be out a lot, then this is not the dog for you.

They are great with kids; I don't think they ever really grow up themselves, so kids are their idea of heaven. Occasionally their strong willed 'mind of their own' can make them conveniently deaf: if they decide they want to bring you a present there is no persuading otherwise. Their drive to retrieve and carry has no bounds. Our house keys now have great clanky things attached, since Teddy and Tango do love bringing you all your personal items; phone, keys, shoes, some more shoes, television remotes etc…

Cockers like to 'chat', however the girls are far worse than the boys. Male cockers can do a sad low pitched howl if they feel left out: great at sounding the alarm at every new sight and sound. Their barks are more chatty 'yips', designed to get your attention and to make sure you act on it.

Maintenance wise they have a much fuller coat than the female cockers. They have more feathering through the tail and legs, and can have a handsome chest of soft hair. However they are not great shedders of coat, and just require a brush to keep them looking top notch.

So to sum up: great family dogs, but also a loyal companion for everybody. They do love company, and though they can go and have a snooze in their bed whilst you are out, they would much rather be with you, even if it means just going for a drive in the car. They are very versatile, we know a lot of people who use their Cockers for a running companion (when they are old enough and fully grown), they can sit on your feet whilst you type and are always up for a game of ball or playing with the kids. They are very social animals and inclined to make their voices heard; whether it be complaining you have gone out or telling you there is someone at the door. Hence they are not the quietest of creatures! But practically perfect in every way.

Pros: always happy and pleased to see you. Good with kids of all ages. Loves being involved in family life.

Cons: can be noisy and need to be kept mentally stimulated. Very sensitive to harsh voices, you need to be calm and controlled if you need to discipline.

Cocker females

The 'Diva' of the group, stuffed full of character, which overspills in a burst of energy as they throw themselves into your arms, snuggling up against your body and entwining their love and passion for you in an excited bundle of fur.

They are the most high maintenance dog of the lot. But goodness me you get value for money, there is so much energy and love squished into a small snaky body there is no wonder it has to come out at such velocity and eagerness.

They are very sensitive to voice, needing a calm firm

authority to keep their naturally rather naughty nature under control. They are very human in character, you will certainly know if you have done something wrong – brilliant at sulking- though giving them a cuddle usually makes them forget their troubles. It needs to be noted that they do tend to be more interested in getting what they want as opposed to what you want! As long as you keep that in mind, then there will be no problems.

Like their male counterparts they are very vocal. In fact, more vocal, it is not a bark or a howl, just an excited 'yip'. This is carried out in a rather like morse code fashion, direct eye contact with you is the more desired feature, and off they go.

But, as with everything else, there is always an exception to the rule. In our case, it is the beautiful Bay. She is a stunning deep red cocker girl, much chunkier in body than the other bitches and a calm soothing soul. She does not bounce, she glides. She does not bark, more a deep throated clear of the throat. Bay is loveliness personified. She produces solid and cheerful pups that waddle round spreading glee to anybody they meet.

All cocker girls are great family pets, and get very attached and protective of the family. In some ways that is a great plus since they are like a canine au pair, but it does need to be watched. Our black cocker Jade is always on high alert if new people come into the house. Small she might be, but no one would ever doubt that she would fight tooth and nail to save her spawn (and that certainly includes my daughters).

The cocker girl's main downfall is that they like to be the centre of attention as long as it suits them. They are very good at ignoring any of your directions but do have the decency to look guilty. A springer girl on the other hand would just totally ignore you, no qualms about that!

They are always following you around – usually in front of you so you trip over them. They like to know exactly what it is going on. Cocker girls are a mixture of being full on queen of the castle, and 'don't bother me I am having a nap'; As long as you can keep above them in the pecking order, they are a good all round pet. Opinionated they might be, feel that jumping in and out of downstairs windows is an easier access to the great outdoors and stealing your socks, you get bundles of character in the littlest of the spaniels we are talking about in this book.

Pros: you will always know where they are! Happy and chatty and truly part of the family.

Cons: great aptitude for barking and making themselves known.

Cocker colours:

You have a huge choice here. Brown which can be more a chocolate colour or heading towards liver (darker than the chocolate). Gold, fox red (not recognized by Kennel Club but take a look at our dogs, Bay, River and Tango), Lemon, orange and blue roan, black and white, liver and white, red and white. Cockers do not breed true regarding colour and virtually any two parents of any of the colour combinations can produce any colour scheme within the same litter.

3 THE SPRINGER SPANIEL DEFINED

Springer males:

In the long run these are the most stoic, solid and dependable dogs we have ever had. As long as you can get through the early years of sometimes intense naughtiness, it is like child-birth, the memory of their sometime unspoken deeds just gets washed away. In character, they are the lowest maintenance of all the dogs we are talking about. I am sure there are plenty of bonkers Springers out there, we keep getting told there are, but in my book, that is just a fallacy.

The boys are incredibly loyal, love human companionship, happy to settle by your feet in any chore that you do. They appear to be snoozing, but one eye is partly open and an ear gently cocked, just waiting to see if you move away. They then will stumble after you, and collapse again at your feet.

They can be great diggers, not all of them though. I have spent years bellowing at Billy, but Bobby never has never once dug a hole. Billy loves chewing toys and underwear. Bobby, for his part, just hides his personal favorite thing of the day and guards it from other dogs.

You will hear so many tales of how a springer male is intuitive to illness. They are completely in tune with your body, even if you don't know it, they do. None will leave you if you are unwell, they will make your bed their own, and stay with you come hell or high water. They come and find you if you are upset, eyes bulging with worry, they hate raised voices and will often hide in those scenarios.

They can get crotchety in their old age, but nothing worse than having a grump and hiding behind a sofa. Some are terrible chewers but this can be handled, they are good at opening doors, whether it is a food cupboard or a back door. Some howl when they think they are alone, but soon will stop and curl up and sleep. Very patient with children, and if start to get hassled too much, they have the sense to disappear and hide up. In essence they are great family dogs, nothing more to say!

Pros: very loyal and great family dogs, Quite happy to be the only dog in the family, treating owners with respect whilst remaining great companions. Not great barkers but will tell you if visitors appear.

Cons: some are inclined to dig and chew whatever they feel like on that particular day.

Springer girls:

The springer girl is a little more enthusiastic about 'stuff' than their male counterparts. They like everything to be in the right place, and if it is not, then they are quite determined to tell you. Bubbles gets quite furious if someone props a parcel up by the front gate (seasoned delivery people are not put off by this barking ball of fluff and just march down the drive), or an unknown car parks in the layby opposite us. This she particularly dislikes if it's getting towards night – obviously feels that this is a threat to the family and needs to be seen off. Which she does: with great aplomb.

We have two very different character traits in our Springer girls:

First we have the working women: shorter legs and body than the others, a more freckled coat and wavy ears. These girls are constantly wagging their tails with delight at seeing you. Always wants to play. Not howlers or great barkers, just an excited yelp at seeing you. Their tails wag so much; it looks like they are powered by their undulating rear ends. I am constantly followed by a crocodile line of springer girls; if I change direction suddenly I find myself in a sea of girls all greeting me as though I have been away all day.

It doesn't mean they have to be working (i.e. shooting or field trial dogs) in this sub category, just that they will need more bouncing around, having balls thrown for them and long, interesting and varied walks. They are perfect for a family who loves being outdoors and active. They do love the indoor life, they know the best spots in the house and where the sun falls gently in a corner on an autumn day.

The other characters are the Queens of all they survey: soft coated, bigger bodied, gentler in nature. All the Springer girls are great Mothers, who love rearranging their puppies in bundles and piles. Very keen to move their pups onto a nice soft bed, the moment your back is turned.

They love a walk and play, but it is not their reason for being. They loved being loved. Blue are oldest springer bitch will gently tug on your jumper for attention, she used to lead my youngest daughter around by her wrist, her mouth softly over Matilda's skin, she would guide her to wherever she wanted to be; a sofa or towards the larder for a quick snack. Never once has she hurt a soul, visitors might not always see her in the kennels, she only comes out to be admired on a one to one basis and then she charms every person she meets.

The other quiet girls sit snoozing in the sun watching the workers bounce around, but when you take them out for a walk you see another side of them. Not vigorous like the workers, but elegant and lithe. Always conscientious of checking where you are so they don't lose you. I truly believe they feel as though they are looking after you and not the other way round!

A springer bitch will always give you interesting value for money whether you prefer the more bouncy ones, or the laid back girls. They are sharp eyed, remember exactly where everything is, and just love you. What more could you ask?

Springer girls – 'busier' ones

Pros: great confident and fun dogs, always up for a play. Ready and quick to learn, easily integrates into a bustling family life

Cons: don't always know when to stop and do require the commitment of daily walks in a variety of places.

Springer girls – 'quieter' ones

Pros: Will always 'mother' your family, gentle and kind hearted, loves being out and about with you but also happy to be left alone.

Cons: can be quite determinedly attention seeking when they want a cuddle or a fuss. Prone to getting quite chunky since they can like food as a priority and exercise a bit further

down the list!

Colour combinations:

English Springers are most likely to be either black and white, or liver (brown) and white. However you do also find tri-coloured Springers, white with black and liver markings.

4 THE SPROCKER SPANIEL DEFINED

Sprocker males:

A solid robust force of nature. That's all I really need to say. However that's probably not enough! It must be noted that Sprockers, like all other dogs take their characteristics from their parents. A Sprocker who has Blue or Bubbles for a mum will tend to be quieter, ones that have Izzy or Sky as Mother, are busier and we would sell as such.

Sprocker boys are big men; they grow into their adulthood quickly after a slow start. For the first three months they are smaller than the Cocker or Springer pups, and then…off they grow at a quite alarming rate. Due to this reason, I would personally surmise, they don't really know their own strength. They are heavier set than both their counterparts. Yet still, frighteningly agile. It can be an overwhelming combination.

They need to be handled with a firm consistent authority and touch right from day one. Otherwise you are going to have a big dog on your hands who gives you no respect. There seems to be a common misconception that a Sprocker male is going to be smaller than a Springer. This can be entirely false. Again it's down to the parents and the combination of gene pools. Ernie our 'Sprocker at stud', for example, is bigger than his Father Ted, and virtually the same size as our two male grown Springer's.

However as long as you show him who is boss, you will have the sweetest dog you could imagine. They have very deep eyes, sometimes blue for first few months and then they deepen in colour. Their coats are heavy but require less work than a Cocker male.

Ernie spends most of his life gazing wistfully at my right pocket. This is where the treats are sometimes kept. Not that he has had any for over a year, but he still ponders over that pocket. He is a gentle soul, very compliant to his vigorous Father (though he is actually bigger than him now). With this gentleness comes an enthusiasm for life which can be overwhelming (even to me) on a bouncy day.

They need a chance to let off steam and then they settle down. Male sprockers can also be broken down into the same categories as the Springer girls. Ernie's Mum is 'Sky', one of our working girls. She was born to be busy, hence so is Ernie, but she has a very gentle nature deep inside, take her in the house and she curls up next to you on a chair, periodically taking time to sniff your face and neck gently so her whiskers tickle on your skin as she moves.

The long and short of it is that, to get an understanding of a Sprocker male, it is important to look at the parents. By nature they are gentle clever creatures, but need to keep the 'oomph' contained at the appropriate moments. This requires commitment to the dog is in its formative months. However once the groundwork is set, they will be your devoted, well behaved friend for life.

Pros: kind hearted, great with all family members, not a barker or a howler, fluffy coat but easily managed, does not shed a lot of hair but will need an occasional clip, great dog for agility or working but also good family pet.

Cons: naturally very exuberant, greedy, will need firm handling during training, good at jumping fences, bigger than you might expect!

Sprocker bitches

These are a great combination of Springer and Cocker, nearly every time. They are very intelligent and quick to learn and, like their male counterparts, need to be taught and interacted with properly in their first few months. Putting the ground work in will pay off, this does not mean you are actively training the puppy but you are just setting some rules.

In the most part Cockers develop slower than the

Springers, there is no point trying to train a Cocker until it passes a several month old stage. Springers can be trained to sit, stay and lie down from ten weeks old however please don't think of that as something you have to do! Hence Sprockers inhabit the middle ground. The girls have the bounciness of the Cocker girls but are not high maintenance in character and naturally obedient. They are chunkier in build, but apart from that you could easily lose a Sprocker bitch in a crowd of Cockers.

Our lovely Sprocker 'Flo' was whistle trained the basics in a day. They love being trained and love getting things right, which is a great combination. Sprocker girls can be bossy to other dogs, whether they are siblings or just contempories so it is wise to have a think about dynamics if you are thinking about having two dogs at the same time.

They love kids, being very childlike in nature themselves helps. Instinctively they know how to behave with individuals. Thus they are sensible with young ones and playful with older ones.

Sprockers do need a good walk a day, but like most spaniels they do most of the running around in great loops, whilst you stroll on behind.

Like the cockers they do love to retrieve, this can also mean a bit of a dance to regain ownership of whatever personal item of yours they have borrowed. However they are usually so delighted with their handiwork it is impossible to be cross with them for too long.

Some do have the Springer trait in eating your favorite bits and pieces, but it's not something that happens on a regular basis. As long as you tell them off as firmly as possible, the memory of that indiscretion and subsequent remonstration should see you in good stead for a while.

Pros: happy cheerful girls with easily managed coat. Easily trained by young and old. A good first time family pet.

Cons: can be dominant over other dogs. You will need to keep their very active mind interested as well as their active body exercised.

Colour combinations:

Sprockers are more known for being with black or chocolate with small white markings. However they can always follow the same principle of the Cocker are come in a myriad of colours. So think along the lines of black and white, liver and white, lemon/orange/blue roan too.

5 NOW THE SCIENCE – HEALTH CHECKS

Spaniels can suffer from varying inherited diseases which are specific to their breed i.e. English Cockers and English Springer Spaniels. Having the stud dog health tested will mean that any of the inherited diseases will not be passed onto his offspring, though they themselves might be carriers and if you wanted to breed your puppy then you would need to have your pup health tested too. However if both parents are health tested then their offspring and subsequent puppies will be deemed heritably clear and not going to be at risk for the following diseases:

English Springer Spaniels are tested for:

- Fucosidosis (Fuco)
- Progressive retinal atrophy (PRA)
- Primary Glaucoma

English Cocker spaniels are tested for:

- Familial nephropathy (FN)
- Progressive Retinal Atrophy (PRA)
- Primary Glaucoma

It is not necessarily a bad thing if your pups parents are not health tested, it doesn't mean that their breeder has done anything 'wrong', it just means you will have not the added reassurance that these health tests bring.

When it comes to Sprockers, it becomes more unusual for the parents to be health tested unless they come from a recognized breeder. However sprockers are just as likely to be affected by these inherited illness passed down through their parents (whatever some people say). But the general feeling is that they are a strong and solid breed. Since sprockers are not a recognised breed they themselves cannot be health tested.

Fucosidosis (Fuco)

Canine Fucosidosis is a severe, progressive and ultimately fatal. It is characterized by deteriorating signs of the nervous system that progresses over several months. The disease, which affects young adult dogs (usually between 18 months and 4 years of age), is caused by the absence of an enzyme called 'alpha-l-fucosidosis'. Signs include in-coordination, change in temperament, loss of learned behavior, loss of balance, apparent deafness and visual impairment. This condition (which can affect all English Springer Spaniels whether they are 'working' or 'show' stock) is inherited through an autosomal recessive trail and has been reported by ESS owners and breeders from all over the world.

Progressive retinal atrophy (PRA)

This is a disease if the retina, in which the rod cells in the retina are programmed to die. PRA occurs in both eyes simultaneously and is non-painful. Because PRA makes the rods die, and the rods are responsible for vision in dim light (night vision), the first clinical signs that an owner can notice is night blindness and the pupils are dilated. Owners will also notice a 'glow' and/or increased 'eye shine' from their dog. Unfortunatly the natural cause of the disease is that blindness will occur within a year.

Familial nephropathy (FN)

This is a recessively inherited renal disease, the onset of this renal failure typically occurs between 6 and 24 months of age. Clinical signs may include polydipsia (drinks more), polyuria (urinates more), weight loss, lack of appetite, vomiting or diarrhea. Unfortunately this is a fatal disease.

Primary Glaucoma

Gonioscopy is used to determine how pre-disposed the eyes are to developing primary glaucoma. This is an inherited condition, it usually begins in one eye but almost always (eventually) involves both eyes, leading to complete blindness.

You will find that some breeders do not have health tested dogs, usually because they do not breed on a big scale. Some breeders (like ourselves) have the stud dogs tested so we know that our pups are clear of any inherited illness, and some will have both bitch and stud dog tested. It is always worth asking the breeders/owners if their dogs have been tested.

British Veterinary Association (BVA)

The British BVA, in conjunction with the Kennel Club, offers breeders the possibility of eye testing screen for inherited diseases in certain breeds. By screening breeding stock breeders can use the information to eliminate or reduce the frequency of eye disease being passed on to puppies. These specialized clinics are held nationally on a rotating basis. All health tested dogs need to have their eyes examined yearly and their pedigree papers stamped.

As an owner you too can do your bit to maintain your pups health for the future. Later on we explain exactly what your pup will be vaccinated against, but it is important to stress that your vet can be one of your dogs best friends for life.

It is important that your pup has its first vaccinations at eight weeks old (this should be done by the breeder so the pup has been health checked before you pick him up). Then you should follow this up with the second set of puppy jabs (basically boosting the first lot) between ten and twelve weeks of age.

Your dog will then need to have these vaccinations boosted every twelve months (These must not run over due otherwise you will have to start again). Most vets will send you a reminder card but its worth putting it on the calendar for your own peace of mind.

6 IDENTIFYING YOUR PUPPY

As with most things these days, the internet is the way forward. However old fashioned recommendation via friends or the local vets is also a great way to track down your puppy. There are lots of websites that you can find adverts on: and it is not just the public that advertises on these, you can find local breeders too. We sell most of our pups through the website though and have a waiting list in place for most litters. So a 'google' search for your choice of Spaniel is your first point of call plus a visit to the Kennel Club website if you are looking for a pedigree puppy.

If you are looking for a Springer or a Cocker, it is best to make sure your puppy does come from a 'Kennel Club breeder'. This basically means you are getting a decent genuine puppy and not one who has an unknown past. Though there are lots of good non-pedigree pups out there, it is better to support good healthy and safe puppy rearing and not encourage 'puppy farms'.

Unfortunately there have been lots of cases recently of buyers being duped into thinking they are buying a pedigree

KC registered puppy, but the paperwork never seems to turn up.

So if you are concerned about the authenticity of the breeder being genuinely a member of the Kennel Club then do ask for a copy of the Mother of the litter's paperwork – this will have her KC registration number on it, you can then phone up the Kennel Club (08444633980 option 1 or 2), they are always very helpful and should put your mind at rest.

Sprockers on the other hand are not a recognized breed, so you need to take a little extra care here. A good Sprocker pup will come from a line of Kennel Club registered dogs. Even if the stud (Father) of the litter is a Sprocker himself, he will have had down his line pedigree parents so this is what you need to look for and ask about.

Next step

Before you start any phone calls or visits, you need to decide exactly what suits you. Hence the beginning of this book; so by now you must have a 'feeling' of what you really would like. So now two more things to think about:

Dog or bitch?

Having a bitch will mean that you need to think about her coming into season twice a year. This usually lasts three weeks, and during this time there will be a discharge of blood. This starts off quite light, darkens up and then returns to a light discharge. Most bitches will clean themselves up, some can have almost unnoticeable seasons, but don't be fooled by that, they can still get pregnant. So you need to remember your girl is emitting a highly attractive smell to all the boys in the neighborhood, so you might get a lot of unwanted admirers pawing at your fences!

You can get your bitch spayed which will eliminate all the above drama. Most vets would recommend this and it is done at an early age, usually just after they have had their first season.

Docked or not docked?

This can be a highly contentious subject and I for one, can understand both sides of the argument. Tail docking is highly regulated in England and currently illegal in Scotland. However the University of Glasgow have written a report on a study they have undertaken which basically says that working dogs and/or dogs that have a lifestyle of charging through undergrowth of thorns and bushes should have their tails docked to reduce the risk of injury. If you have ever seen a spaniel with a broken or damaged tail then you would understand the argument for the tail to the docked.

The law now stands that the tail must be docked within 72 hours of the puppy's birth; the owner/breeder of the pup must hold a shotgun or firearms license and the pups will be advertised and sold towards a 'working' market. All of our working dogs and puppies are docked at the kennels. If the litter is destined as family pets then we do not dock the pup.

7 FINDING YOUR PUPPY

If you are going the 'Preloved', 'Petsforhomes', or 'Freeads' route then I suggest you go online early in the day and do your phone calls then. Waiting till the evening means that lots of others will have had a head start on you chatting and making subsequent appointments.

Going direct to a breeder is not so frantic. Please bear in mind that Breeders like us are usually outside covered in mud, and carrying lots of leads. So if you don't get an answer to the phone call, then always follow up with a text and an email. It is better to look enthusiastic in this case. Even if they cannot help you this time with a pup then a polite breeder will at least get back to you and tell you so and maybe offer some helpful advice of where else you could look.

Be prepared to travel - A good puppy from good parentage is worth a few hours driving. Avoid bringing your children for the first visit. In fact, avoid telling them at all to begin with. You need to make sure it's the right breeder and right puppy first, and your kids will only get very excited and make you forget all the questions you wanted to ask (this is from years of my experience!). If they don't know you are even going to see a puppy then they can't get their hopes up....or nag you for weeks...

Be prepared to wait - The right pup is not going to fall into your perfect time schedule. If you have holidays and family commitments booked then the pup will need to put on hold until you have enough quality time to give your new dog a head start in their new life.

We often get lots of phone calls at the beginning of the school holidays asking if we have any pups. If this is the best time for you then you need to be working well ahead of yourselves. You cannot expect to get the right pup at the right age, a few weeks before you want it. Aim on looking six months ahead of yourself. Get on a good waiting list with the assurance there should be a pup in that litter for you.

A decent phone call is essential - you need to have a few questions to hand (easy ones) that can lay the foundation of when you meet the owner / breeder and the puppies. A quick note regarding the Father of the litter – a lot of breeders won't always have the Father of the litter as their own dog, many will use stud dogs from reputable (hopefully!) breeders or people that just own stud dogs. So it is not uncommon for you to be only able to see the Mother with the puppies.

Here are a few suggestions of what to ask:

- Will I be able to see the Mother (dam) of the litter? If the answer is no then just put the phone down with a polite 'goodbye' – never see a pup without its Mother.

- Can I see the Father (sire)? If not, who is he and who owns him?

- Are the parents Kennel Club registered?

- How old are the puppies now?

- When are they ready to leave?

- What do I get for my money?

The last question might seem a bit rude, but you need to know that the puppy will be vet checked and inoculated at eight weeks by the owners vet. Ideally you want to know your pup was vet checked at birth. I would also only go for a puppy that was going to be vet checked and given their first vaccinations by the breeder. That is responsible dog breeding. Many small things can go wrong, none of which you should be dealing with. 'Flow' murmurs in the heart are often detected at the eight week vaccination vet check. These are 99% likely to have disappeared by the last ten to twelve week check and final vaccine.

However you are owed the option of taking that risk or not by the people you are buying from. We (in the case of a flow murmur) always insist on keeping the puppy until the next vet check and second lot of vaccines.

There are also various schools of thought that puppies should be leaving the litter and making their arrival in their new 'home' well before the eight week vet check and vaccine in order for them to bond and socialize more readily with their new owners. I appreciate that this is some people's opinion, but it is not mine. We make sure the last two weeks before the pups eight week check and vaccine is full of safe socializing and fun with all the members of the household, pups get safely introduced to the sounds and sight of traffic and general palaver, housework, dinner time, lots of children and other animals normal daily life can bring. The last couple of weeks before the eight week vaccine are vital ones here, we even keep the pups for another week after their vaccine and microchip keeping up the same daily routine, it is about at nine weeks (though it can change from litter to litter) that we feel the pups are ready to leave us, with a good foundation, and move forwards to their new lives.

If the puppy has been docked, the breeder legally has to have the puppy micro chipped by a vet (not by the breeder- some people are licensed 'implanters' like myself but I am not allowed to chip docked dogs by law). You also have to be given (by law) the original legally docked certificate signed by the vets.

I know this is lots to think about. But it is important for you to be aware of all of this from the beginning. There are lots of corners that can be cut by breeders, and it's important that you begin your journey (even from the first phone call) knowing as much as you possibly can.

On the other hand (sorry) to know too much can also be a burden. Buy a few well chosen books, don't surf the web too much and speak to a few considered people and then make your own mind up. Then you should be ready to meet your potential new pup.

Meeting the pups:

Appearances do matter. Have a look round where the pups are kept. If they are in kennels, it doesn't matter if it is not all brand new, but does it look clean and looked after? Puppies and kennels do have a certain smell, we get used to it at ours, but is should not be overpowering. If they are inside the breeders home, a subtle glance will tell you how well the pups and mum are being cared for. The water bowls should be full and clean. Bedding should be so clean that you would happily sit on it yourself. There should be no leftover crumbs of food on the floor, and the area they are in should look safe and cared for.

Whatever people say, puppies don't choose you. You choose them. They can be a little shy to begin with. Not all pups will come bounding over to meet you however well socialized they are. You smell and sound different to their normal 'humans' and some will sit in the corner observing you. And, when they decide you look and sound ok, they will wander over to say hello.

Obviously some will bounce over to you, but what I am saying do not be put off by the quieter ones, they are just cautiously considering their opinion of you. I like the fact that some pups (and subsequently dogs) have the ability to think before they act.

Make sure you meet the mum. Some bitches are quite happy letting you be around their offspring. Some are rather worried about it. This does not reflect on the mother's character or on the pup's character as they grow. Just watch her with her pups; if they all look happy and contented, then all is well. However if the mum is overly aggressive or downright nervous this can be an inherited trait, so you would need to take some caution at this point.

Now is the time to ask all your questions. If you are a novice it is good to know how much back up you will get from the breeder once you have taken the puppy home. Even if you are a seasoned dog owner, it is a good feeling to know you will have some guidance on your foray into spaniel world for the first time.

If a large percentage of the litter has already been sold, and you have only one or two choices, please do not have the mindset that there is something wrong with the ones that a left. There isn't anything, it's just 'one of those things'. Our black and white Springer 'Bubbles' was last of her litter, and so was 'Ted' our gold cocker, and they are the most perfect dogs we could have asked for!

All puppies will be treated and looked after equally well by a good owner, and sometimes having less of a choice makes life a LOT easier when it comes to picking out your pup.

It is perfectly normal to be asked questions by the owner. They do need to know what experience you have with dogs, where you live, and how much time you have to look after their puppy once it leaves home. In fact, I would be more worried if the breeder doesn't seem interested in you!

Do expect to pay a deposit for your puppy. This is to show your commitment to the pup and to the breeder. Make sure you get a receipt with an agreed final total to pay written on it and signed. At this point you just need to double check what you are getting for your money. So be quite clear in asking.

Lastly don't be pushed into anything. If it doesn't feel right, then walk away.

8 PREPARING FOR YOUR PUPPY

You don't need to spend a fortune on pup accessories, but of course a bit of self-indulgence is always nice if you can afford it. However your first goal is safe proofing your house and outside areas which should take first precedence over everything else.

Sprocker's, Cockers and Springers are intensely nosy creatures, bearing in mind their sense of smell is over a hundred times better than our own, what they can't see, they can certainly sniff. So just because they cannot see something does not mean they don't know where it is!

Family meeting first and foremost since all the members of the family need to agree on boundaries for your new dog. These are the places your dog is allowed to go, and more importantly NOT allowed to roam. Everybody has to agree since everybody needs to make sure all the rules are kept. I found with my kids, the best way was to explain what would happen if baby Bubbles ate through the wires on the back of my computer. The horrified faces are still in my mind, but it worked. Once Billy the Springer started eating Barbie dolls legs, the kid's bedrooms were also declared a no-dog zone, and they managed to regulate these themselves from quite a young age.

Upstairs or downstairs?

Are you going to let your dog upstairs in your home? A lot of people (probably quite sensibly) consider bedrooms out of bounds. A nice, freshly made, soft bed is a great incentive for a grubby dog to fall asleep on. Tango the Cocker loves stealing bed socks (just for the fun of it) from under pillows and will use any excuse to crawl under a duvet and fall asleep. So as you can see I don't ban the dogs from upstairs, but that is a personal preference.

So if upstairs is out of bounds then you need to put a visual barrier across the stairs. There is no point using child gates. In my experience all spaniels are very good at getting their heads in between the bars and then thinking they are stuck. This leads to a howl like you have never heard before, scaring the socks off every member of the house and leaving small children traumatized for life as they watch their beloved pet apparently immobilized for life. The dogs recover quicker than the family by the way.

Puppy gates are widely available and are perfect for the job. Then all you have to do is teach everyone to make sure they shut it behind them. Good luck with that one.

When you have decided which rooms are dog rooms, you need to go on an 'accident is waiting to happen' inventory on your hands and knees. There are plenty of places a puppy can get wedged (and just when you think they will have a learnt a lesson, they go and do it again). So off you go thinking like an inquisitive puppy. Down the side of the cooker, behind the fridge, they at good chewing through electric cables in a trice, and cupboard handles look very inviting to chew (especially if you last opened them with food on your hands).

On a serious note pups can also get collars caught around cupboard door knobs, and can quickly strangle themselves. Hence we take collars off all dogs when they are indoors. The same accident can happen around curtain ties and blind pulls. These need to be put out of the way so they cannot wrapped around a dogs neck. A lot of dogs are great at opening cupboard doors with their paws so child locks are useful here.

If you live near a busy road, its best not to let the dog roam near the main front door. All dogs are easily distracted and last thing you want is to come home after a hard day, open the door and have your dog charge out. Please do not rely on visitors to shut your gates either. However much a sign reading 'please shut the gate' should work, it doesn't.

Laundry/utility rooms can sometimes be a good dog bed area, however electric wires must be nowhere near the ground and you have to make sure your lovely clean laundry is not hanging in a tantalizing fashion anywhere near your pup. Washing machines and tumble dryers can be very noisy and frightening to a young dog and you also have the possibility of the pup crawling into an open machine unnoticed.

Personally I would recommend the kitchen. They are usually the soul of a home, got the right flooring and close to water and dog feed etc. Put a puppy gate up by the doorway, and you can leave the door open when you are not in there, and the pup can watch what's going on in the rest of the house at their own (safe) leisure.

The great outdoors

All spaniels love a good smell, especially one that they can roll around in. So your garden needs to be a completely isolated space where only you and your dog can wander. However Spaniels don't always agree with that idea, and if they can't go over they will try and go under. Hence the garden needs to be inspected on a hands and knees type affair. I have learnt my lesson a couple of times now, and it is totally petrifying to not be able to see a puppy/young dog but be able to hear them squealing for your assistance. I am not going into details but please block up any spaces between garden buildings, make sure any burrows of any kind are filled in and your fences are high enough.

If you feel your garden fences are too low, this can be remedied by adding an extra line of tape, bunting, colored string etc at a jaunty angle. This has been tried and tested here so we are sticking with it as our best form of defense. If it stops Ernie (Wise) the chocolate Sprocker – it should stop most determined Grand National inspired Spaniels (with the possible exception of Maud).

'Maud' owned by Julian Hammond. The irrefutable proof that Sprockers can fly…..

There are quite a few poisonous plants for dogs that quite a few 'normal' gardens will have, the best bet is the 'Dogs Trust' website, they have a great list for you to work through.

www.dogstrust.org.uk

Now a note about fruit trees: Just be aware that a lot of spaniels (mainly Cockers and Sprockers at our house) are good fruit pickers. It is considered a great sport throwing yourself at any low hanging branches, grabbing them, and giving them a good shake. And, of course, eating whatever spoils fall off – this can lead to rather runny tummies.

The Dog Loo

If you wish to avoid using your lawn as an outdoor dog loo then there are ways around this. Decide where the pups outside loo area will be. Preferably somewhere this is already concreted or flag stoned.

The idea is that you make this into an outdoor puppy pen, the place he routinely goes after every meal, and is left there until he has done his business.

The best way to begin with is to put him on a lead, and walk him to the area. This is not playtime so try and keep everything as low key as possible. The split second he starts to wee etc, then praise him calmly. As long as you take him to the same place after every meal he will quickly learns that this is his place for the toilet, not the garden or house.

Vets

Next job is to locate the best vet. If you are a first time pet owner then it is best to begin by seeking advice from another dog owner. All dog owners love talking about their animals, so if you don't have neighbours and friends to ask, then I suggest you find yourself the local dog walking venue and accost (and make friends of course) with other dog owners and walkers.

There is a lot of competition between vets now, since most places you will find at least two separate vet practices. Personally I like the smaller vet groups, where you can actually get to see the same vet most of the time and the vet himself gets to know your dog. Due to this competition you should expect great customer care when you phone up and when you visit. They will want to know your details, your dog's date of birth and some point they will need to know what vaccinations your pup is being given at eight weeks old, this info you can get off your breeder.

Pup classes

If you are planning on puppy training classes, the same applies as above. These classes get VERY full so think and work ahead on this one.

Crate

This has become very popular with puppy buyers. I can't remember it being around when we first had Harry (our original Spaniel), and I have to say I was not too keen on it in the beginning. We do 'crate' train pups for people here, my theory is that if they get used to going in and out of a crate from their earliest memory it becomes second nature. We ask all puppy buyers to supply us (and their pup) with a blanket or towel which we keep in the crate, this then becomes part of their everyday life so when they leave they take 'blanket' with them to their new home and crate.

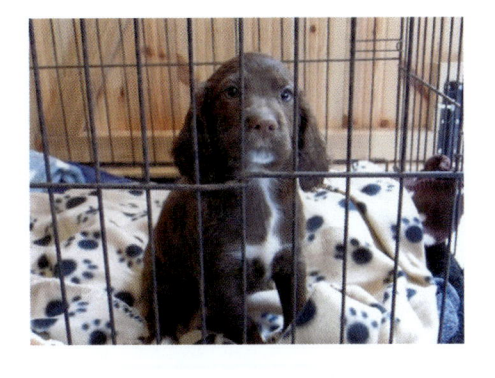

Having done this type of crate work over the last few years I have come around to the benefits of it. It is a good (portable) place for a pup and a dog to call their own, a sanctuary for them to retreat to if need be. It is also a great safe place for you to put them if you need to suddenly rush out.

I used to use my daughters to help with the crate training, whilst they were small enough to get inside one, if caused great merriment from the pups to have free rein and a play with the girls. Sadly they are both too tall now.

So if you are going to use a crate, then it needs to live inside your pups 'safe area'. We suggest putting the pup's bed inside it along with their smelly blankets, around this (outside of the crate) some newspaper for 'accidents' and a water bowl (and subsequent food bowl).

I think a lot of people's negative view on crates is that they look like a cage, a prison for your pup. It is never intended as that, and must never be treated as so. You cannot just put him in there if he is misbehaving, it will have a long term opposite effect. His crate is his castle, however you also need to give him lots of fuss and chat when he is in 'his' area. His crate and space is for his privacy, and apart from if he chooses to go in and have a moments snooze, then (apart from nighttime) he should not be in there for more than a couple of hours a day, and certainly NOT all day!

Around the home

If you have had a puppy/dog before then you can skip this bit! Basically puppies and young dogs (and sometimes those who should know better) can take a shine to things they are not supposed to. However there is no point in telling them off after the fact since it is completely meaningless to them. They need to be caught mid-misdemeanor and verbally told off in the deepest gruffest voice you can muster. High pitched squealing does not cut it. They also do not like being made eye contact with, so it's a combination of deep cross voice and eye contact. You are very likely going to feel a bit silly but it does work.

In their defense we must note that dogs do not have hands (obviously), so they tend to use their mouths to pick up and investigate whatever looks vaguely interesting. However what, when and why is still a lesson to be taught. Bringing you your underwear is not always what you want to happen when you have visitors....

In the meantime here are some potential red rags to your little bull:

- Loo rolls – such fun!

- Tablecloths dangling their edges off the side of the dining / kitchen table....magicians might be able to whip away a cloth leaving the table still covered with your best china. As far as I have discovered, puppies and dogs cannot.

- Play-doh and Lego – one soft and one crunchy (makes for interesting poo).

- Work papers, un-read magazines, homework, un-opened letters, books...these all shred delightfully well.

- Ear-rings – these can be chewed off you and swallowed in a trice by any self-respecting puppy (yes from your ear-lobes).

- Dangling necklaces and long hair. Both of which should be kept well out of a dogs way.

- Oven gloves and tea-towels….never there when you need them…

- Sticky yummy children's fingers and face and any child gesticulating whilst holding food. This easily leads to tears.

- Shoes, all very sweet when your 9 week old pup undoes your laces, but when you are in a hurry to get out finding only one school shoe does not help your mood.

This phase does not always happen; some pups are practically perfect in every way. Some, however, are a little naughty for a short while.

Car journeys

We have found crates to be the most perfect method for car journeys. To avoid too much stress on my part (simply because I still struggle with putting up dog crates from folded) we have one in the car on a permanent basis. This means that if I go on the school run I can easily take one of the dogs or pups with me 'just for the experience'. The more a pup and young dog get used to traveling in a car from an early age, the quicker (and better) do they get accustomed to the motion and noise of car travel.

In past I have had a car with a dog guard permanently in place along the back of the boot shelf. I can categorically say that virtually all our dogs (including the enormous German Short Haired Pointer) have wriggled through the dog guard and landed beside me one way or the other. Very pleased with themselves too. I am sure lots of other people have dogs that behave in a normal fashion. Ours do not.

Dogs can travel on the backseat, or in the foot well of the passenger seat. These can be safe as long as someone sensible has hold of the dog, or the dog is wearing a canine seatbelt. I do use a seatbelt on some of the dogs, others mange to get their legs wound and trussed up in it and whilst I am untangling them (having pulled over of course) I usually end up with the dog sitting on my lap in front of the wheel.

A final word of caution: Please make sure your car windows are not down too much, I do know someone who has lost a dog out of the window whilst driving along. Both dog and person where fine – but they were lucky.

The best bet is the crate though, from my experience. Have one big enough so that it is almost wedged in the boot (i.e. limited movement) and have a soft bed or mat inside the crate for comfort and cushioning. Heaven forbid you have collision, but 'just in case' means you want the crate to be firmly held in the boot, and the dog to have some cushioning in the crate.

A lot of dogs do suffer from travel sickness. And there are remedies you can buy over the counter at large pet stores. Otherwise you can always speak to your vet.

It is better not to leave a dog (or pup) in a car if you can help it. But if you have to, then make sure you are parked in a shady spot, the windows are open enough for fresh air but not enough for a determined dog to wriggle out of. Do not leave your keys in the ignition, since dogs are very good at jumping on inside car door locks and centrally locking the entire car. Hence leaving them in a crate is a better and safer way forward.

Things to buy

<u>Collar</u> - However excited you are, I would suggest not going too over the top to begin with when it comes to a collar. Pups are very good at taking their collar off, chewing and shredding them in a thrice. If you have the inclination to order a bespoke handcrafted leather collar then it is best to wait till the pup is fully grown. You have been warned. All dogs now must have an identity tag on their collars by law. I would not put your dog's name on it (just in case someone takes a fancy to your beloved for themselves, the last thing you want is to give them any help finding out your dog's name), but just put your name, and as many contact details on as you can.

<u>Lead</u> – we use a very light weight lead attached to the collar for training purposes. We attach it and then letting the pup potter about with it on with us watching very carefully from the sidelines. So to begin with you just need a lead that attaches nicely to your collar with a sturdy clip. Nothing too long or you will end wound up around your knees, lampposts or trees. Once you have got the learning to walk on a lead sussed you then have a huge quantity of differing types of lead to choose from.

<u>Crates</u> – as mentioned previously it is worth buying two whilst you are at it, one for the car and one for the home. The one for the car can be a bit smaller, but please make

sure your boot will shut with the crate inside before you buy it. It sounds obvious but it is one of those things easily overlooked. We let our puppy buyers try out some of our differing crates in their car, makes life much simpler for all! The one for the home can be as big as you like, but do make it cozy inside.

Water and food bowls – non slip bowls are your best here. Once your pup realizes that food and water bowls are delightful fun when empty (or not) and helping them wiz and clang across a floor makes a LOT of noise and gets a LOT of attention from you, your life will then come a bit more chaotic than need be. Stainless steel might not be the most prettiest but they are the hardiest. You can also buy specially shaped bowls specifically for spaniels, these are cone shaped and designed so floppy ears don't fall in food (and they actually work!).

Uggeshall Luna Eclipse…. the Empress of emptying water bowls…owned by the Raymond family.

Bed – start small at first so it feels cozy and make sure you can machine wash it. So material yes, whicker no….pups love shredding wicker.

Toys – you really need too many of these. Our favorites have been Kong toys, balls on ropes, cotton rag toys and things to help with their teething. Avoid squeaky toys, they will drive you mad and are not particularly safe if pup manages to open it and swallows the squeaky thing.

Food – make sure you have what the breeder is feeding the pup. Either buy some from them or make sure it is stocked locally. You don't want to run out on Christmas Eve and find yourself frantically driving round looking for obscure dog food. Of course, you might be better organized than I have in the past but I am sure you get the gist.

Grooming kit – spaniels are very good at self cleaning, the sides of sofas are a wonderful place to drag one's body along, and freshly made beds just 'super' for a muddy pooch. In all fairness though, spaniels don't need much grooming, just a weekly brush with a soft brush and a bit of a comb through the lovely feathers they have. We do recommend buying a flea comb (for the 'just in case' moment), for the parents amongst you a head lice comb can double up as a flea comb in absolute emergency (and vice versa but don't tell my kids that). There are lots of lovely dog shampoos on the market, some smell delicious, however baby shampoo is a good substitute.

Other bits of kit…..

Poo bags – these are very essential for you when you start walking your pup in public places. The general public can get VERY cross if you are seen to not be picking up your dog waste. You can buy poo bag pouches which you can attach to your lead – these are a very good idea. We use nappy bags if we can't get poo bags, but they are not as strong and therefore more likely to break.

Treat bags – if you are planning as using treats as a training aid then just shoving them in your pocket is not a good idea (here speaks the voice of experience) since they just end up a mass of moldy crumbs. You can buy specially made bags from pet stores, or just improvise.

Dog food bins – these are made to take a large bag of dog food, have clip down air tight lids and a scoop. So far none of our dogs have managed to break into one so I would say are quite reliable!

That's it - you should be ready to go now

9 LIVING WITH YOUR PUPPY

Bringing puppy home:

You need a small bag of emergency equipment for the drive home. We normally don't feed our pups in the morning they are leaving (morning is the best time) to eliminate the chances of vomit. But bring a couple of towels, plastic carrier bags and some wet wipes to mop up any spillage.

Morning is best so you can have a whole day settling your new puppy in. It is also best for there only to be two of you in the car, I appreciate that homecoming is a big thing but you don't want to overwhelm him with too much excitement and noise in one go. The passenger should put a towel on their lap, puppy on the towel, holding on firmly. I would recommend putting a collar and a lead on the pup and having the lead wrapped round your hand. This is so your slippery puppy doesn't decide to take a nose dive towards the driver or an opening door. You can put your pup in your car crate, but once you have done that you need to commit to keeping him there for the whole journey. So if he cries, howls or whimpers you cannot take him out and comfort him otherwise you are teaching him the lesson that if I cry, I get attention and what I want! So if you have a long journey then I would suggest having pup on your lap for part of it, and then putting him in the crate if you want to.

Once you reach home, offer him some water and then take him to his outdoor loo, and calmly wait until he has a wee or suchlike. Lots of praise, then indoors to his new abode.

Now is the time to introduce him to his bed/crate with the nice smelling blanket from him mum and siblings. Using a hot water bottle, filled with hot water from the tap and then wrapped in his blanket is extremely comforting for all pups. Put him in and walk away. Hopefully the excitement of the day so far combined with the smell of home will let him have a nap.

By now, if there are children involved, the excitement of the expected arrival of their new pup will have reached fever pitch (unless they are young teenagers and they might be excited but refuse to show it). BUT the puppy's introduction to any children must be as low key as possible. Get the kids sitting down and let the pup approach them, when he is ready. Give the kids a small tempting treat to have on the palm of their hands to give the puppy, hence making it all a good experience all round. Now explain that the puppy needs some quiet time of his own to explore, understand and settle down in his new home. Bribery usually works for me, a magazine with various freebies or something else to keep them busy.

Since I am sure you have all agreed on some puppy rules, now is the time to remind everybody and mention that the pup does not need to be picked up at every available moment, he will begin to feel rather nervous if this keeps happening and start to back off at the sight of feet coming towards him. Also it is good to remind smaller people that once the pup is having a snooze or in crate then he is not to be disturbed – maybe they can go and make various 'DO NOT DISTURB' signs etc. for a little bit. That might keep them busy and get the concept drummed into their subconscious!

Now you might have introduced all the other human members of the family but there can also be a few non-human inhabitants too. The most likely is the cat. Felines can often take a dim view of the new kid on the block, especially if they have been in residence for quite a while. However some cats love dogs. Maybe not straight away but they can form a fabulous bond (deep sigh of relief all round). Our cat Dick loves having a wash from any passing dog. Bubbles takes quite a while in cleaning his ears, paw gently on his chest, ears turned inside out and care and consideration taken.

When you first introduce your pup to the cat, it's the pup that needs restraining not the cat. If you have a bolshie feline, he will probably hiss and give your pup a wack round the nose if he gets too close. Strong minded cats get very indignant that a young odd looking up-start even dares to consider interfering with him. And that, hopefully, is the end of that.

If you have a more nervous cat, then it is going to take a little bit longer. You will need to teach the pup not to dart and try and play with the cat. The best idea is to distract the puppy every time he tries to go after the cat, so he is not tempted to give chase. Pups must be taught that cats are not for chasing at all costs. So it will be an ongoing lesson, puppy in the room with the cat, pup on lead to begin with, when he starts to go after the cat, distract him and start playing – this should hopefully teach him that cats are not to play with (but humans are) and the longer he doesn't chase the cat, the less likely he is to think about it as he grows older. So two words – RESTRAIN- DISTRACT.

The rest of the day should be spent relatively quietly but still keeping him up and about (you want him as tired as possible for his first night away from his siblings). Show him round his new home, but only the parts he is allowed in and get started with your house training. Put him to bed as late as possible having taken him outside for a final toilet. Then shut the door, walk away and put a pillow over your head. Some pups can shriek like the world is ending all night, some pups just go to sleep as if nothing has changed.

You do have another option for the first few nights – however you do need will power of cast iron for this one. It is very hard for a pup, used to being with his siblings, to suddenly be left alone in a new space with recently introduced companions. Having the pup in your bedroom is a gentler introduction to his new life. But this does not mean the pup in your bed, but down in his crate/playpen with a refreshed warm hot water bottle and blankets. When he starts to whimper you can say a few reassuring words and then let him get on with trying to sleep in his new space. If you think he is whimpering because he needs to go to the loo, then you need to get out of bed, take him outside with minimum interaction, then bring him back him up and place him in his space while you quietly go to yours. After a few nights he should ready to try and sleep on his own – there are going to be points when he is left by himself so it is a valuable lesson that he learns that he is not always surrounded by family.

The first few days – begin to house train

Routine, routine and some more routine. This is all about basic house training and general good manners. What work you put in now makes a huge difference; the adage 'start as you mean to go on' was invented for puppies.

Once mum has left our pups (for the majority of the time), we start the process of training to newspaper. If you choose to do so, start collecting old papers early. We are lucky in the fact that all my Mothers friends plus other kind hearted souls hoard their used papers for us and they appear over the main gate in bundles on a regular basis. This usually leaves me catching up on world news on my hands and knees in the puppy kennel.

There is also the option of puppy pads you can buy at big pet stores. I would like to add that the record for shedding those to pieces is held by Jade's Cocker pups in 2013. It took about 30 seconds to shred and much longer for me to clear up. We are sticking to paper.

The idea is that you cover your floor area that the puppy will inhabit with thick layers of newspaper (this is why kitchens and other non-carpeted rooms are best). Every time the pup wakes up or has been fed, put the pup on the paper and try and keep him there until he has relieved himself, lots of praise must be forthcoming. You then pick dirty paper up and then replace with clean.

As soon as the puppy gets used to the idea of the paper, he will run to it to relieve himself, again more praise. Very slowly you start to reduce the amount of paper, moving the paper area towards the door. In the long run, and with Mother Nature being nice, you would aim to have the kitchen/outside door open with some newspaper on the threshold and just outside the door too.

 If you start toilet training outside too, this should all fall into place neatly. Just keep an eye on him after eating, hopefully he will start to gravitate towards the paper, at which point you whisk him outside.

You do need to stay with him though. A Spaniel will be mightily miffed if you take him outside and just leave him there. He is expecting to be kept company and to find the back door shut in his face, will just result in basic whining, no going to the toilet, and then coming in and relieving himself indoors.

The first few days - Feeding

Now food manners: always keep his water bowl clean and full so he can drink whenever he wants and he always knows where it is. I would advise putting it in a corner in the kitchen, otherwise family members are inclined to kick it over and swear at you for leaving said article in a stupid place. Some Spaniels do also have a habit of emptying water bowls so they can carry them round…..

His first meal at home is important. Before you put the dish down, let him sniff the dish and then lick a bit from your fingers (you might need to wet the food down a little if you are on pure biscuits). He needs to see you as the Fairy Godmother of the food bowl (or Godfather etc.) and that you are in charge.

Attempt to get him to sit: if you move your hand over his eye line, puppies do tend to sit down. Then place the food in front of him. If he doesn't finish it (which is quite unlikely) then just take the remainder away.

It is now you need to keep him either on his newspaper if you are paper training, or outside if you are going straight to the outdoor method. Keep him moving about a little, but focused on toilet not play. When he finally goes, lots of quiet praise WHILST he is doing it. Ecstatic praise is saved for the really clever stuff like 'sit' or 'stay'.

At this young age he will still be on three meals a day. So you will find your life revolving around feeding, playing and getting on with the house training. Your perseverance will pay off so don't get disheartened.

The first few days – walking and grooming

The best thing is to get pup used to be being bathed and brushed from an early age. When they are really little we use the kitchen sink, but once they get to squirming size then the bath with a non-slip mat is the best bet. Always try and use a puppy shampoo, otherwise you might find your pups skin gets very irritated.

They do not need a lot of brushing at this point, but it's good to get them used to the idea of it. So use a soft brush all over his body once a day will get him used to being fully handled and will stand you in good stead for later in life.

Walking

A good rule of thumb is for your puppy to have five minutes per day per month of age: so a three month old puppy would have five minutes x 3 equaling 15 minutes walking. You can do this twice a day. Pups do get bored of being in the same place, that's usually when they might consider tunneling out and seeking adventure elsewhere so do think 'variety is the spice of life' for your young Spaniel.

You can use this walk time as part of their socialization process. The more your pup sees at a young age the better. He needs to be introduced to absolutely everything you can muster. Start on quiet roads, and work up to busy noisy ones. Chat to policemen (missed this one out with Bubbles so she now woofs rather aggressively at any poor policemen. We have had a rather embarrassing moment when she got a young officer cornered in my Mothers bedroom....), firemen, postmen, people on bikes, horses that are being ridden, motor bikes and anything else you can think or and / or find.

Your first attempts at walking on a lead are going to be haphazard. So deep breath and don't expect to get very far. The main point is to be consistent. Some puppies fly off at 100 miles an hour, some puppies just spread eagle themselves on the ground and refuse to move.

Lots of reassurance is needed from you. Some treats in your pocket. Try to walk the pup between you and a fence, a wall or a line of trees so you have a narrow corridor for the pup to keep to. Keep the lead short and upright and gently persuade the puppy that walking beside you is the safest option.

Your goal is not to let the puppy pull. So basically every time the pup pulls away from you, you stop. When you stop the pup will usually turn to see why he can't move forwards anymore, making the lead slacken. At this moment you immediately praise him and then continue walking for as long as the lead stays loose.

The process is then repeated. And probably repeated a few times more. However your patience will be rewarded in the long run, the more effort you put in now, the easier everything else will fall into place.

Letting puppy off the lead

This always worries a few of our new puppy owners, the idea of letting the puppy off the lead, and then he disappears off into the distance never to be seen again. As far as I know it is has never happened.

You need to think of yourself as the pups replacement pack. After spending some time with you, the puppy will consider you as their 'safe house' and not run off from you.

'Coco' owned by Lucy Hollis and family…..here she is contemplating the great outdoors.

In the meantime (in between vaccinations for example) you

can work on your recall about the home). Start in the same room as the pup, treats in your pocket, call his name and show him the treat and he will coming running to you (you can start using your whistle here too – more information on whistle training later on).

When he arrives in front of you, lots of praise and a treat and so you carry on. You can work up to being in other rooms, top of the garden wherever it is feasible for you pup to find you from. As he gets better, less use of the treats just keep up the praise.

If you are still worried about letting him off in the big outdoors, then retractable leads are your way forwards for a little while. It won't take long for trust to be built up and then you can go for a 'proper' Spaniel walk which entails them running ahead and then circling back just to check you are too not far away!

Recall

When we are training our pups we always use a whistle as well as verbal commands. This is so our pups and dogs come back to a pure whistle but also their name, which is vital since I often go out without my whistle.

However whistle training is great for various reasons:

First it saves your voice, it travels much further than your dulcet bellowing can, and it's short, sharp and effective and will hide any trace of negative emotion in your voice.

You can also train to sit and stay at a distance, which

always looks good. It means that the dog will always respond to the whistle, so it doesn't matter who walks him if he is pre-programmed to come back to that particular pitch

NB whistles come in different pitches. It is advisable to just buy a couple of the same one to begin with (it does not matter which pitch) and keep one as a spare. It you are going to be really clever and later on you have more than one dog, you can have a different pitch for a different dog. Then you have to remember to put both whistles round your neck…..and which whistle is which…..

The main thing to remember is to have your whistle around your neck (I do appreciate this sounds obvious but if you are not used to it, it is easily forgotten). As an aside I would like to also mention that our goats, sheep and ponies are also trained to come charging to a whistle. It was not planned like that but it is surprisingly efficient!

So you call the puppy by his name, and then a short sharp two blasts on the whistle. Carry on doing this for a few weeks, and then try just blowing the whistle. If he returns just to the whistle, job done. If he doesn't then you just need a bit more time practicing.

When you have both mastered this, you can go and hide around the house and then blow the whistle. Depending on your hiding skills you might need to call a few times…but he will find you (and be very pleased with himself).

In the meantime you can also work on the 'Sit' command. There are two options here:

First have a titbit in your hand, with the pup as near to you are possible. Show him the titbit up high, he should naturally sit to look up to you. As he does this, say the word 'Sit' as his bottom hits the ground. Lots of praise and the treat ensue.

Second way is minus the treat. Have the dog standing as close to you as possible, if you hold your palm out over his line of vision he should naturally sit to be able to look up to you, and regain eye contact. Same as before, as his bottom hits the ground say the word 'Sit' and lots of praise.

You can now start bringing in the whistle too if you plan on using it. As you say the word 'Sit' follow immediately with one short sharp burst of the whistle. I find it easier to have the whistle in my mouth between my teeth whilst I do this.

Preventative and general health care:

These are basically things to do on a regular basis to help keep your puppy/dog healthy and avoid any unnecessary trips to the vet.

Ears –Spaniels have beautiful ears but they can cause problems. Checking they are clean and / or cleaning them weekly makes a big difference. First thing to do is have a quick smell. If they smell foul then it's a trip to the vets: they might have an infection and bacteria in their ears.

It is good to get your Spaniel used to having their ears cleaned once a week if you can. Never use cotton buds or cotton wool. You need to use the flat cotton pads that 'one' would use for make up or taking off nail varnish.

You should be able to get a good ear cleaning solution from your local pet store. For the first few times, start by just giving your puppy a head massage, incorporating his ears, so he gets used to the idea of you feeling all around and in his ears.

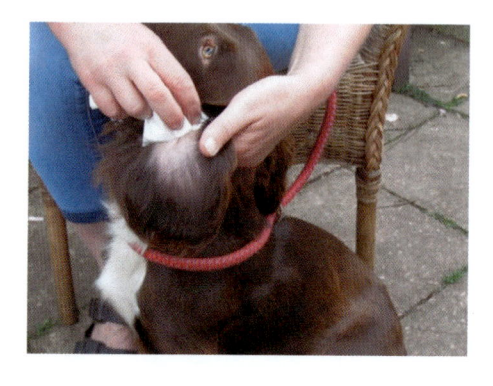

When you think he is ready gently pull the ear flap upward to straighten out the ear canal, and then squirt some of the solution into your puppy's ear. Massage the base with your fingers for about 30 seconds (you should be able to hear it squelching), making sure the cleaning solution gets deep down into the ear.

At this point your puppy is going to be desperate to have a good shake of the head to get rid of that solution out of his ear. Keeping hold of him (i.e. collar and lead job, you don't want him running off), let him have a little shake before you start cleaning with the cotton pad (you might want to pull yourself back a bit at this point, canine ear solutions don't taste very nice and sting your eyes).

Use a damp cotton pad to gently wipe out the dogs ears and clean them as best you can. Make sure you don't poke anything down into the ear itself. All you need to do now is make sure they air dry! So preferably out and about in the fresh air.

If you don't feel confident doing this yourself the first time, then it is worth asking your vet to show you how to do it.

If you notice your dog doing a lot of vigorous scratching of the ears, it probably means he has ear mites. This is another vet visit. However a lot of the new worming tablets now encompass worms, fleas and ear-mites so it would be worth paying a bit extra for the future when you next have to worm your dog.

Do keep your dog's ears brushed on a regular basis, the hair in this area can so easily get knotted and tangled and pull on itself, causing discomfort. You can trim with sharp scissors the hair on the inside of the ear flap. This is best done once you can trust your dog to stand still. Sometimes a second person to hold onto him whilst you do something like this will make the whole process a lot easier.

Eyes - eyes are so delicate on any of us so if you are ever unsure what is going on with your dog's eyes, then it is a vet visit. The one ailment you can deal with is Conjunctivitis; this is the term for inflammation, discomfort and reddening of the eye often most noticeable by the eye weeping, or being partially closed up by a thin film crust. You can use boiling water with salt, wait for it to cool down to body temperature and using a cotton pad gently soak the eye, removing slowly the puss or crust.

Worms

Roundworms: all puppies should be wormed fortnightly from two weeks to three months of age, then monthly up to six months of age. After that your pet should be wormed twice a year.

Tapeworms: These need a guest pass (hosts) which is usually given by your dog's fleas (if they have any). Hence using a multi worming tablet (we use Stronghold) which keeps different types of worms at bay, as well as fleas and ear-mites. It might be a little more costly but it is certainly worth every penny.

Fleas

As long as your breeder handed you over a flea free puppy, this is all about prevention rather than cure. If you use the multipurpose worming tablet, which also combats fleas, you should not ever have a problem. You do need to keep any eye on other dogs if they are visiting your home; fleas are very good at jumping from one dog to another!

If you did invest in a flea comb, then it's certainly

worthwhile having a 'flea-check' when you groom your dog. Fleas like to hide down by the dog's tail, around the collar area and if you turn your dog belly side up, you might be able to see a few scampering away from the lower belly / genital area where the coat is finer.

We use a flea comb and a bucket of tepid water, gently but firmly pull the comb through the coat (we start on the belly up side) and then dunk any fleas or grit in the water and then comb again. If there are fleas, they will scurry off into the thicker part of the coat, so you turn the dog over and comb through there etc.

In the warmer months all our dogs go swimming in the river in the field, this is a great way to give the dogs a simple clean and to help fleas float away. Washing with shampoo is something that needs to be done only now and then, you don't wish to clean the coat of too many of its essential goodness.

Vaccinations

Vaccines are basically a modified live, or killed, form of the infection which does not cause illness in the dog, but instead stimulates the formation of antibodies against the disease itself.

The five major diseases are:

- Canine distemper
- Infectious canine hepatitis
- Leptospirosis

- Canine parvovirus
- Kennel cough

Many vaccination courses now include a component against parainfluenza virus, one of the causes of kennel cough, which is not a good thing for your dog to have at all! A separate vaccine against bordetella, another cause of kennel cough can be given in droplet form down the nose by your vet. Your dog will spend the rest of the day glaring at you, but it's worth a sulky Spaniel so you can rest assured that you are vaccinated up to the hilt.

Puppy should have their first vaccination at 8 weeks approximately and a follow up dose 2 to 4 weeks later. It is at this point you can have the separate kennel cough vaccine. After that you need to have your dog booster jabs on a yearly basis. Most good breeders will not let their puppy's leave until they have been vet checked and had their first lot of eight week vaccines.

Feeding and dog treats

A good food for your dog will bring health and happiness all round. There is no point in feeding your beloved Spaniel a poor quality food. However some of the medium priced brands that you can buy in the Supermarkets can do just as well as some of the high price bracket ones you might see sold at your vets.

With any luck your puppy will not require any specialized food types however quite a few dogs can be wheat and gluten intolerant and this can differ from one pup only in an entire litter. This also might be something that doesn't become apparent until the puppy starts growing up.

We use a very high quality, sensitive puppy and junior food for the first six months. It is wheat and gluten free and packed full of everything your puppy needs to grow in every sense. We find it is usually when the puppy/young dog moves from a junior food to an adult food that such intolerances can become apparent.

Changing from one brand to another needs to be done slowly otherwise you will end up with runny stools and an upset stomach.

Do not worry about feeding the same food to your puppy all the time; puppies are not like us humans when it comes to food stuffs so they won't get bored!

The amount you feed your puppy each feed time is an individual calculation based on the puppies weight and should be based on the manufactures guidelines which will be on the bag itself.

They need to be on three meals a day up to about nine months and then down to two. Some people will then cut this down at about eighteen months to one meal a day but that is a personal choice for you. Our dogs get two meals a day; we just split the amount they should be having per day into two.

There are two main popular types of food you can give

your puppy now. Firstly is the dry complete dog biscuit which has everything in it your pup and dog will need. Secondly (and gaining momentum in interest) is the raw food diet. This is simply raw meat, bones , fruit , vegetables, raw eggs and sometimes dairy all ground up and frozen in containers. They have been quite controversial, but the popularity is rising. The idea is that dogs will thrive on an evolutionary diet based on what canines ate before they were domesticated.

Potential risks which have been mentioned is a threat to human and dog health from bacteria in raw meat, and that this unbalanced diet (in their eyes) may damage the health of the dog.

What is boils down to for you, is that use whichever feels most sensible and right for you.

Treats

There are lots of treats on the market, from the supermarket to the vets practice. It does seem to be that some people feel you shouldn't need to use a treat to train a dog, or to reward him for good behavior.

I like giving the dogs a treat. For good behavior, doing what they are told and just simply because it makes me feel good too! I make our own dog treats and then freeze them. However that doesn't mean I don't buy a supermarket packet every now and then.

And finally…

You should be all set now for a great life with your puppy, here are some ideas that you can work towards if you would like to do a little bit more with your trusty canine.

<u>Agility</u> – dog agility measures the handlers ability (or not!) to direct their dog over a course of varying obstacles

<u>Companion dog shows</u> – these are fun informal events that all dogs can take part in to help raise money for charity.

<u>Local dog shows</u> – last one I did of these Bubbles was the naughtiest dog ever and finally conked out snoring and refusing to wake up under the kids face painting table. However apart from that embarrassing moment they are usually good fun!.

<u>Field trials</u> – these have been developed to test the working ability of gun dogs in competitive conditions.

<u>Flyball</u> – fast, furious and fun. This is a growing sport involving a knock out competition. It is very popular at Crufts, so watch out for it.

<u>Heelwork to music</u> – competitors devise routines up to 4 minutes long and perform with their dog

Obedience – this is testing how obedient and well trained your dog is…..

There is lots more information, help and guidelines on the Kennel Club website: www.thekennelclub.org.uk

~

Both Richard and myself wish you many happy years with your spaniel(s). Good luck!

ABOUT THE AUTHORS

Anne-Marie Millard and Richard Botwright own and run 'Uggeshall Kennels' in North Suffolk. From here they breed working Springer's, Cockers and Sprockers as well as train young part trained dogs.

Anne-Marie is an established author with eight already internationally selling non-fiction books translated into 12 differing languages.

Richard is an ex gamekeeper with decades of experience in the shooting and dog training world.

They live at their small-holding with Anne-Marie's children and Mother, creating a three generation household under one roof. Combining this with various other animals wandering round, it is a great place to gain insight, information and to spend both their working lives and personal days with their shared passion of the Spaniel in all its shapes and forms.

21814932R00046

Printed in Great Britain
by Amazon